Law & Grace

From Shadows to Reality

Jesten Peters

Published by Keys of Authority Ministries Inc.
www.keysofauthorityministries.org

Keys of Authority Ministries Publishing is committed to publishing works that give glory and honor to the name and work of Jesus Christ, and provide keys to advance Christians in their walk with Him. The company's foundational scriptures are Matthew 16:19 and Ephesians 4:11-16.

ISBN: 9798218497866 (Print)
ISBN: 9798218497873 (EPUB)

RELIGION / Christian Living / General
RELIGION / Biblical Studies / General
RELIGION / Christianity / Pentecostal & Charismatic

Table of Contents

Dedication

I am dedicating this book to all those who imparted to me a love of studying the Word of God—the Bible.

My earliest recollections are of my mother, Georgia Porter Harman, reading the Bible in front of me, and to me and my siblings.

After our family moved from War, West Virginia, to Detroit, Michigan, we attended the *Church of God Tabernacle* located at the corner of Connor and Mack on the east side of Detroit. Our pastor was Luther Turner. He had such a distinctive voice and was a wonderful pastor to our family. What I remember most about his sermons was when he would say, "Don't take my word for it, go home and study it to make sure I am preaching the truth." He was always encouraging the congregation to study the Bible for themselves.

I had wonderful Sunday School and Vacation Bible School teachers as a child. Their love for the children they taught and the Bible have influenced me all of my life. One such teacher was Doug Scoggins in my early 20s. He could take you deep into the Word.

I also need to mention Kenneth Hagin, Sr., and the wonderful teachers I had while attending *RHEMA Bible College* in Broken Arrow, OK. Bob Yandian was one of those instructors. Buddy Harrison was another one. They had such a wonderful way of sharing the Word that it literally came alive as they taught.

I was in my mid-20s when I was first introduced to Dad Hagin and then *RHEMA*. Even though I had a good foundation from my childhood, there was so much more to study and learn. I had never heard about our authority as believers.

I can still remember Dad Hagin saying something like this, "Keep a teachable spirit. Don't ever think you know it all, or that you can't learn more." This is so true. We should continually be learning. When we stop learning, we stop growing and become stagnant.

And the greatest teacher of all, the Holy Spirit. What a treasure we have been given.

I want and desire to know more—and therefore I follow in the footsteps of those who have made a lifetime of study.

"For the law is only a <u>shadow</u> of the good things to come, not the <u>realities</u> themselves. It can never, by the same sacrifices offered year after year, make perfect those who draw near to worship."

Hebrews 10:1, Berean Standard Bible (Emphasis added)

Acknowledgments

I am thankful for every person who has unselfishly poured into my life the love of Jesus Christ. Also, to everyone that helped make this book a reality, especially Holly Payne VonWald, whose talents and dedication brought this book to life. To my brother, Pastor Ronald Harman for reviewing the book and offering additional scriptures for the manuscript. And finally to those who cover us in prayer and support the ministry of *Keys of Authority Ministries, Inc.* My prayer for them is always for God's abundant blessings to overtake them.

But most of all I want to thank My Heavenly Father for giving His Son Jesus Christ to die for our sins. For in Christ's death on the cross, and as a result of His resurrection, He defeated Satan and took the keys of death, hell, and the grave from him.

For those of us who have accepted this free gift of salvation, we possess the keys of authority over our enemy. May we learn to use the power and authority we have been given by the Holy Spirit to further His Kingdom for *"such a time as this."*

"Now the <u>first covenant</u> had regulations for worship and also an earthly sanctuary. A tabernacle was set up. In its first room....was called the Holy Place. Behind the second curtain was a room called the Most Holy Place....the priests entered regularly into the outer room to carry on their ministry. But only the high priest entered the inner room, and that only once a year, and never without blood, which he offered for himself and for the sins the people had committed in ignorance. The Holy Spirit was showing by this that the way into the Most Holy Place had not yet been disclosed as long as the first tabernacle was still functioning...—<u>external regulations applying until the time of the new order</u>."

Hebrews 9:1-10, NIV *(Emphasis added)*

Introduction

Before there was Grace, there was The Law.

The Law has been described as:

Law – the revelation of the will of God set forth in the Old Testament; the first part of the Jewish scriptures; PENTATEUCH, TORAH.

I think of it as the requirements to set up the appearance of The Messiah, who was to come and redeem mankind after the fall by Adam and Eve in the Garden.

I guess you could say I have been a "Law and Order" junkie. I do not watch much television, because most of it offends me. We have gone downhill with the kind of programs that are produced now. However, I do like to watch true crime stories. I usually can figure out what has happened before it is revealed in the program. I think I would have enjoyed working the detective part of solving a crime.

I try to look at reading scripture as a type of detective work. As the scriptures in Isaiah 28 says, "*...precept upon precept, line upon line, here a little and there a little.*"

From *Dake's Annotated Reference Bible KJV*: "precept Hebrew *tsav*, injunction; commandment; precept. From *tsavah*, enjoin; appoint; charge; set in order. Literally mandate must be upon mandate, mandate upon mandate; line (Hebrew *qav*, a rule; measuring cord) upon line (rule upon rule); here a little and there a little."

I was raised in a Christian home and attended a Pentecostal church. I so appreciate the teaching I had as a child and teen. But when I got into my 20s, I was introduced to what is called "the Faith movement" and began to learn about studies in the Hebrew and Greek words that the scriptures were written in. I had no idea about any of this. In fact, I didn't know that the Old Testament was written in Hebrew, with a small portion in Chaldean, and the New Testament was written in Greek.

As I studied more, I came to realize how hard it is to translate correctly, or shall I say *completely*, from one language to another.

I learned that the King James is not the all-in-all. However, I became aware of a study Bible that allowed me to learn more about Hebrew and Greek words. That Bible is the *Dake's Annotated Reference Bible (King James version text)*. This Bible has "four equal-sized columns on each page—two of text and two of notes and comments, self-pronouncing text, and a Complete Concordance and Cyclopedic Index."

It was Dake's desire to "give in ONE volume the helps a student of the Bible needs from many books—Bible Commentaries, Atlas, Dictionary, complete Concordance, Dispensational Trust, Topical Text Book, Bible Synthesis, Doctrines, Prophetic Studies, and others." Finis Jennings Dake, the author, had 100,000 hours over 43 years of searching the Scriptures.

This study Bible whet my appetite to learn more. I learned about the Dead Sea scrolls, how the Bible was translated into Latin, and later how English-speaking people wanted a copy in their language. I also learned that the King James Bible was not the first English-language Bible.

I encourage you to study how we received our English Bible. Many people lost their lives, as is referenced in *Foxe's Book of Martyrs*, so we could have the Word of God in our homes. And with the invention of the Internet, it can be Google-searched literally at your fingertips. At the time of the writing of this book, here is a link where you can find the History of the Bible:

https://greatsite.com/english-bible-history/

In your study, you will come across these names:

- Wycliffe
- Tyndale
- Coverdale
- Matthew/Rogers/Tyndale
- "Great Bible"
- Geneva Bible
- "The 1611 King James Bible"

...and more.

Over the years (I am now in my 70s), I have obtained more and more study Bibles and helps. I attended *RHEMA Bible College* in Broken Arrow, Oklahoma, in my late 20s, and later in life, studied for a Bachelor's in my 50s and a Master's in my 60s degrees in Theology. That is not to say that I am an expert—I am not. I just love to read the Word/Bible. I read the complete Bible each year, usually out of a different study Bible, and I learn something new each time I do.

However, as much as I like to read others' writings, I also recognize that the Holy Spirit is the best teacher. I love when He speaks to me while I am studying. It is almost like a light bulb goes off in my head. I underline and make notes in my Bible as I study. Whoever inherits my Bibles and library, I hope those notes and underlines will speak to them too.

The reason for my writing this book is to share some of those experiences I have had. Some may disagree with my thoughts and opinions, and that is okay. Maybe it will stir them to study.

2 Timothy 2:15 in the KJV says, *"Study to shew thyself approved unto God, a workman that needeth not to be ashamed, rightly dividing the word of truth."*

When I am reading each year, I take the first quarter to read and study in the New Testament because that is where I live. I am part of the Church, the Body of Christ. And then I take the last three quarters of the year to read and study in the Old Testament.

The Old Testament points toward Christ—the Messiah and the Redeemer—the One Who would come to fulfill the requirements of The Law. We owed a debt that we could never pay. We were born into sin, but Jesus, the Christ, was not born with a sinful nature. He was the only One who lived a completely sinless life, and therefore, was qualified to pay the debt I could not pay. Words cannot express how very grateful I am to Him.

In the Old Testament, I learned about The Law, but in the New Testament, I learned about Grace.

His Grace, His mercy, His love. There is nothing better.

Jehovah had made a covenant with the children of Israel with The Law. They were to obey The Law and its commandments. However, when we read the Old Testament, we learn they fell short in every way.

Animal sacrifices had been ordained and were to be carried out by the Priests. There was no true redemption by The Law. Its requirements had to be fulfilled. One was to come who would fulfill those requirements.

John 19:28-30 (NKJV) tells us, *"After this, Jesus, knowing that <u>all things were now accomplished</u>, that the Scripture might be <u>fulfilled</u>, said, 'I thirst!' Now a vessel full of sour wine was sitting there; and they filled a sponge with sour wine, put it on hyssop, and put it to His mouth. So when Jesus had received the sour wine, He said, <u>'It is finished!'</u> And bowing His head, He gave up His spirit."*
(Emphasis added)

Jesus declared, "It is finished!"

What was finished? The Old Covenant requirements were completed. He had met them all; He had satisfied The Law and a New Covenant had been established.

Jesus, at the Lord's Supper, instituted a New Covenant and better covenant.

"When He took the cup of wine and blessed it, He said, 'This cup is the <u>New Covenant in My blood</u>, which is poured out for you.'"
Luke 22:20 (Emphasis added)

In referring to the New Covenant, Jesus was announcing that through His death and resurrection, forgiveness of sins would be made available to all and that humanity <u>could once again live in communion with God</u>.

This New Covenant was so important to the Christian identity that the writings of the apostles came to be called the New Testament, another term for New Covenant, while the Hebrew Scriptures were known as the Old Testament, or Old Covenant.

I am going to endeavor to show the difference between Law and Grace, From Shadows to Reality, as I write. I live in Grace—the Reality. I hope you will come along with me on this journey.

I consider my calling and gifting in the fivefold ministry gifts that Jesus gave to the church in Ephesians (apostle, prophet, evangelist, pastor and teacher) to be a teacher. Therefore, I use definitions and other resources in exploring the Word of God.

Disclaimer #1
This book could never contain all that Jesus accomplished with His death and resurrection. It is only a small sampling of it.

Disclaimer #2
During my many years of study, I have made notes to myself from other teachers, commentaries, etc., and failed to record the source. My writings are not meant to plagiarize, or to withhold credit where credit is due, only to share what I believe to be truth.

"I will establish <u>My covenant between Me and you and your descendants</u> after you throughout their generations for an everlasting covenant, to be God to you and to your descendants after you."

Genesis 17:7 (Emphasis added)

"For if that first covenant had been faultless, then no place would have been sought for a second."

Hebrews 8:7, NKJV

Chapter One

Covenants

We could literally spend a lifetime studying the covenants in the Bible, but for time and space I will only touch on a few of the covenants that Jehovah made with His people. Then we will briefly examine the New and Better covenant Jesus made with His blood/sacrifice for all people.

Before we can look at covenants in the Bible, we need to understand what a covenant is and how it is related to The Law.

Covenant is a word we don't use much anymore. In our culture, most of the time, we use the word "contract" instead of covenant.

Covenant in the dictionary is defined as:

Cov·e·nant /ˈkəvənənt/

noun
an agreement; a contract drawn up by deed; a clause in a contract; an agreement which brings about a relationship of commitment between God and His people. The Jewish faith is based on the Biblical covenants made with Abraham, Moses, and David.

verb
agree by lease, deed, or other legal contract

When I hear the word legal, I immediately think of The Law. The dictionary definition is as follows:

Le·gal/ˈlēgəl/
adjective
of, based on, or concerned with the law: or permitted by law.

And when I think of a legal contract, I immediately think "legally binding." The dictionary definition for binding is:

Binding
adjective
a promise, agreement, or decision must be obeyed or carried out.

Synonyms: *compulsory, necessary, mandatory, imperative, compulsory, obligatory, conclusive, irrevocable, unalterable, indissoluble*
Opposites: *free, voluntary, optional, discretionary, unforced, unconstrained, noncompulsory.*

We need to understand that in the covenants/legal contracts Jehovah made with the children of Israel, each party had a responsibility. There are at least two parties to a covenant or contract, and sometimes more.

Jehovah made a covenant with Adam in the garden (Genesis 1:26-30, Genesis 2:16-17). Adam failed to keep his part and lost his home. We still see the effects of that today when we have to work hard to make a living. However, Jehovah made a promise in Genesis 3:15, of a <u>redeemer</u>.

Jehovah made a covenant with Noah and we still see the evidence of that covenant today when we see rainbows (Genesis 9:11).

Jehovah made a covenant with Abraham and in Genesis 22:18 states the whole earth would be blessed because of his obedience. This blessing came when Jesus was born and also has a future blessing attached.

Jehovah made a covenant with Isaac and Jacob, followed by a covenant made through Moses to the children of Israel (Deuteronomy 11). We can still see the effects of this covenant by looking at the nation of Israel and her history.

When studying Deuteronomy chapter 28, we see what each party to the covenant was responsible for. It states if the children of Israel would obey, they would be blessed, but if they didn't, they would bring a curse upon themselves.

The Law was handed down by Moses to the children of Israel. It was a legally binding contract/covenant between Jehovah and the children of Israel.

We see the on-again/off-again obedience of the children of Israel—in the wilderness with Moses, with Joshua, through the period of the judges, and into the period of the kings.

Jehovah made a covenant with King David, which has and will affect us today and throughout eternity (2 Samuel 7:8-16). A member of David's family would have an eternal kingdom, which points to the King of kings, and Lord of lords, Jesus Christ.

Sadly, the children of Israel did not fulfill their part of the covenant and eventually lost the land that Jehovah had promised and provided for them. However, there was a promise they would one day return to their land and become a nation again. That promise was fulfilled on May 14, 1948, and I was blessed to be in Israel on May 14, 1998, 50 years after their rebirth, in what we called their year of Jubilee.

Even though the children of Israel did not fulfill their part of the different covenants, Jehovah was faithful. John 3:16 tells us that God gave His only begotten Son to be our redeemer, to fulfill all the obligation of The Law, so that Grace could be obtained.

Jesus came, born under The Law and all of its requirements, to fulfill The Law and provide us with a New and Better Covenant. A covenant not of animal blood and sacrifice, but by the blood of the spotless lamb of God - sent to take away the sins of the world. All The Law and Prophets were fulfilled in Christ.

*"Therefore the law was our tutor to bring us to Christ,
that we might be justified by faith."*

Galatians 3:24, NKJV

Chapter 2

Types and Shadows

In the Law of Moses, we see many rituals and requirements instituted. There is disagreement as to the exact number of laws given. The number 613 is used by many, and is divided into positive, "do this" commandments, numbering 248, and negative, "do not do this" commandments, numbering 365.

Tip for Further Study
If you would like to study more on this, visit:
https://www.gotquestions.org/613-commandments.html

No one, past or present, could perfectly keep all The Law, with the exception of Jesus. It was always meant to be a means to point us to Christ. The Law was used to show man their need for a savior. The Law was not and is not our savior.

The Law could not save us.
The Law could not redeem us.
The Law could not justify us.
That is why we need Jesus.

If, by keeping The Law, we could be saved and redeemed, then Jesus would not have needed to come and die for us.

Matthew 5:17-18, NIV, says, *"Do not think that I have come to abolish the Law or the Prophets; I have not come to abolish them but to <u>fulfill</u> them. For truly I tell you, until heaven and earth disappear, not the smallest letter, not the least stroke of a pen, will by any means disappear from the Law <u>until everything is accomplished</u>."* (Emphasis added)

Through His life, death, and resurrection, Jesus fulfilled all of God's righteous commands. Mankind was not righteous, but Jesus was.

From the dictionary, righteous means:

Right·eous - adjective
1. (of a person or conduct) morally right or justifiable; virtuous:
Similar - good, virtuous, upright, upstanding
Opposite - wicked, sinful, unjustifiable
2. very good; excellent:

ATS Bible Dictionary defines Righteousness as:

"Rectitude, justice, holiness; an essential perfection of God's character, Job 36:3; Isaiah 51:5-8; John 17:25; and of His administration, Genesis 18:25; Romans 3:21,22; 10:3. It is the wonder of grace that as the righteous guardian of the law, He can acquit the unrighteous. 'The righteousness of Christ' includes His spotless holiness, His perfect obedience the law demands; and 'the righteousness of faith' is that imputed to the sinner who believes in Christ. With reference to personal character, righteousness is used both for uprightness between man and man, and for true religion, Genesis 18:23; Le 19:15; Isaiah 60:17; Romans 14:17; Ephesians 5:9."

Jesus came to fulfill The Law.

According to the dictionary, fulfill means:

Ful·fill *verb*
1. bring to completion or reality; achieve or realize (something desired, promised, or predicted):
Similar - succeed in, attain, realize, consummate
Opposite - fail in
2. carry out (a task, duty, or role) as required, pledged, or expected:

From Dake's commentary, we see that the Greek word, *plero*, means, *"to satisfy, expire, and to end by fulfilling like other prophecies when fulfilled - Mt.1:22; 2:15, 17, 23; 4:14; 8:7; 12:17; 13:35."*

From the dictionary, accomplish means:

Ac·com·plish verb
1. achieve or complete successfully

There was only One who could come and fulfill the requirements of The Law, only One who was righteous, only One who could justify, and His Name was and is Jesus.

As a side note, we call Christ by the name Jesus. Jesus is actually the Greek word for Yeshua. Jesus' name in Hebrew is Yehoshua, which, over time, became contracted to the shorter Yeshua. The name Joshua/Jehoshua is the same as the name Jesus. There is no letter "j" in Hebrew, instead it is a "y". The name Jehoshua/Yehoshua means "Jehovah is Salvation." There is salvation in no other one but Jesus.

The Law could not save. The Law was not righteous. The Law could not justify. The Law could only point us to the coming Savior, the coming Redeemer, the One who could fulfill and accomplish what was required. His Name is Jesus (Yeshua).

According to the dictionary, justify means:

Jus·ti·fy - *verb*
1. show or prove to be right or reasonable:
Similar - give grounds for, give reasons for, give a justification for, show just cause for
2. declare or make righteous in the sight of God

From Dake's commentary, we see the Greek word, *dikalosis*, means, *"the Act of God declaring men free from guilt and acceptable to Him and counting them righteous (Rom 3:25; 5:18)."*

In the Garden of Eden, Adam and Eve were created perfect. In fact, they walked in the Garden *with* God. They had perfect communication and communion with Him. But when they sinned, that communion was broken. There had to be a way to bridge the gap that was now between man and God.

In Genesis, we see the first promise of how that gap would be bridged. The promise was given in Genesis 3:14-15, NIV:

> *"So the Lord God said to the serpent, 'Because you have done this, Cursed are you above all livestock and all wild animals! You will crawl on your belly and you will eat dust all the days of your life. And I will put enmity between you and the woman, and between your offspring and hers; He will crush your head, and you will strike his heel.'"*

Satan's seed or offspring would constantly try to destroy mankind and would be instrumental in the crucifixion of Jesus. By the death of Jesus, Satan thought he had conquered because he held the keys of death, hell and the grave. However, Jesus would use the cross and His death to humiliate Satan, take the keys from him, and be raised from the dead with the keys.

Colossians 2:15, NKJV, says, *"Having disarmed principalities and powers, He made a public spectacle of them, triumphing over them in it."*

In Revelation 1:18, KJV, Jesus proclaimed, *"I am He that liveth, and was dead; and, behold, I am alive for evermore, Amen; and have the keys of hell and of death."*

From the foundation of the world, God had a plan. He knew mankind would sin. He knew mankind would need a savior, a redeemer, a sacrifice to fulfill the righteous demands, to justify mankind, and to bring us back into full communion with Himself.

Jesus was always the plan. We see that in John 1:29, NKJV:

> *"The next day John saw Jesus coming toward him, and said, 'Behold! The Lamb of God who takes away the sin of the world!'"*

Hebrews 10:1, NIV, explains, *"For the law is only a <u>shadow</u> of the good things to come, not the <u>realities</u> themselves. It can never, by the same sacrifices offered year after year, make perfect those who draw near to worship. The law is only a <u>shadow</u> of the good things that are coming—not the <u>realities</u> themselves."* *(Emphasis added)*

Old Testament types, shadows, patterns, symbols—we could study these for months—but I'm just going to touch on them. A "shadow" is sometimes called a secondary light. When I read this, I thought of the Moon reflecting the light of the Sun. That type or shadow is not the true light, but just a reflection of it.

A "type" is a divinely purposed illustration of some truth. The Greek word *typos* means "example." And a "shadow" is not the "very image of the thing," for a shadow is out of proportion, and is an imperfect representation of the thing it reveals. So, the Old Testament "types" are "shadows" in the sense that they are not the "Real Thing," and are but imperfect revelations of it.

In the next few chapters, we will look at some of the "shadows" in The Law that would become "realities" in Jesus Christ.

PASSOVER AND UNLEAVENED BREAD
"On the fourteenth day of the first month at twilight is the Lord's Passover. And on the fifteenth day of the same month is the Feast of Unleavened Bread to the Lord; seven days you must eat unleavened bread."

Leviticus 23:5-6, NKJV

THE FEAST OF FIRST FRUITS
"And the Lord spoke to Moses, saying, 'Speak to the children of Israel, and say to them: 'When you come into the land which I give to you, and reap its harvest, then you shall bring a sheaf of the first fruits of your harvest to the priest'".

Leviticus 23:9-10, NKJV

Chapter 3

Passover, Unleavened Bread, and First Fruits from the Dead

When we study the Hebrew Feasts and Festivals, I believe they are showing us about His appointed times. These three early spring holidays can easily be shown as shadows of the realities to come because Jesus fulfilled all three.

While I do not personally celebrate the Hebrew feasts/festivals, I do like to read about them, especially from writers who are Jewish Believers in our Messiah, Jesus Christ.

I wanted to share with you websites where you can study more about these feasts/festivals, and where I have shared from.

Resources for Additional Study:

- https://hebrewrootsmom.com/the-feast-of-unleavened-bread-vs-passover-whats-the-difference/
- https://hebrewrootsmom.com/first-fruits-an-offering-out-of-faith/

I recognize the significance of Passover and have attended a Seder to get a better picture of it. I would recommend attending a Passover Seder at least once in your life, especially if you are a serious student of the Bible.

I believe the Lord's Supper/Last Supper became our Passover meal, and instead of celebrating one time a year, we can celebrate His covenant meal every day.

The Shadow/The Law
Passover

While often referred to as such, Passover isn't a week or even a day, but a meal held on the 14th day of the month of *Nisan* on the Hebrew calendar. This corresponds to a date in March or April on our Gregorian calendar.

It's important to note here that we follow the Gregorian calendar, and not the Jewish calendar. Thus, this explains the reason for the difference in dates for Passover and what I call Resurrection Sunday.

Although the original command can't be kept since it includes the sacrifice of the Passover lamb at the Temple, an annual celebration allows us to remember what God did for His people in Egypt.

The meal for Passover, called a Seder, isn't merely to nourish those who partake, but to serve as a memorial to what God did for His people in the Exodus from Egypt. It's to be eaten on the 14th day of the month of *Nisan*, at twilight. It's important to note here that days on the Hebrew calendar start at twilight the night before.

The Reality/Grace
Jesus, Our Passover Lamb

The Passover lamb in Egypt foreshadows Jesus, our Passover Lamb, and this is clearly shown during the Seder. Just as the blood of the Passover Lamb rescued the Hebrew people from slavery, it's the blood of Jesus that saves us from the slavery of our sin as well.

1 Corinthians 5:7, NKJV, tells us, *"Therefore purge out the old leaven, that you may be a new lump, since you truly are unleavened. For indeed Christ, our Passover, was sacrificed for us."*

The Shadow/The Law
Unleavened Bread

The Feast of Unleavened Bread is to start on the 15th day of *Nisan*, the same month as Passover, at twilight. This is a 7-day feast, and the first and last days are to be Sabbaths. These Sabbaths differ from the weekly Sabbath (Saturday) and may occur on any day of the week. Which day of the week they're on changes from year to year but, no matter what day they occur on, the same rules apply as for the weekly Sabbath—rest and keeping the day holy.

The command for this feast says to eat unleavened bread for seven days and to remove all leaven from your homes before the feast begins. This is the period where the Feast of Unleavened Bread overlaps Passover.

The Feast of Unleavened Bread gives those who participate in it such a great picture of the sin in our lives! The Bible often uses "yeast" or "leaven" to signify sin.

The Reality/Grace
Jesus, No Sin Was Found in Him

This is the part of this feast that points us right to Jesus. When we see how difficult it is to get all the leaven out of our homes, we realize just how difficult it is to get the sin out of our lives. It's easier to get the big, obvious sins out of our lives, but more difficult to get the hidden ones out.

Even though we can't get all of the sin out of our lives, we have Jesus to cover them all. Though we should still strive to live in a way that pleases God, if we believe in Jesus as our Savior, He even forgives the sins we'd rather leave in the dark places.

This is why we need Jesus! He's the only one capable of perfectly cleaning the "homes" of our lives, which allows us to have a relationship with a holy God.

The Shadow/The Law
First Fruits

Just after Passover and during the Feast of Unleavened Bread, First Fruits (or *Yom HaBikkurim*) is a celebration of God's goodness to His people and to give thanks for what He's given us. The feast is an offering of the first fruits from the harvest.

A High Priest would wave a barley sheaf before God, starting the Counting of the Omer, the 50 days from First Fruits to Shavuot/Pentecost. Offerings were then brought to the Temple, specifically a blemish-free lamb, flour mixed with oil, and wine.

The Reality/Grace
Jesus, First Fruits From The Dead

First Fruits was the day Jesus rose from the dead, as Jesus died on Passover three days before First Fruits. But it's not just a coincidence that He rose on First Fruits. Jesus rising from the dead on this day also confirms that He's the first of the "harvest" to come, the first to defeat death.

Paul referred to Jesus as the First Fruits in 1 Corinthians 15:20-24. Through Jesus, we have life, and that life will be resurrected through Him. How? Romans 8:11 tells us that it's through God's Spirit living inside us. When Jesus died, the Bible tells us many people were raised from the dead! They were to be a First Fruits offering of sorts.

Jesus rising from the dead is the most important thing we can celebrate as Christians! By not staying in the grave, Jesus showed that He is the Son of God and genuinely has power over even death itself!

Jesus' resurrection was the First Fruits of the Harvest. I'll talk more about harvest in the next chapter on Pentecost.

But first I wanted to share some thoughts on Ephesians 4:8, which states, *"Wherefore He saith, When He ascended up on high, He led captivity captive..."*

Theologians differ on the meaning of this verse. Some believe it means "a band of captives," "a multitude of captives," the foes of Christ, the devil, death, the curse, and sin (Colossians 2:15; 2 Peter 2:4), led as it were in triumphal procession as a sign of the destruction of the foe.

Others believe it means those believers who had been held captive in Hades/Sheol/Hell until Jesus came to free them.

The Translators New Testament translates the scripture this way:

"This is why Scripture says, 'When He ascended to the heights, taking a host of captives with Him, He gave gifts to men.'"

Dake's Annotated Reference Bible KJV notes state: "He lead a body of captives to heaven, like an earthy conqueror. Some were the many that were resurrected after Christ (Mt. 27:52-53), and the rest were the immortal souls that were not resurrected, but merely liberated from captivity to Satan."

To me, the imagery here is a conquering hero. He has taken the spoils from the enemy. He has rescued those who had been locked up in prison, unable to be free. And He has taken the ability of the enemy to capture those freed again. He has disarmed the enemy, taking the enemy's most powerful weapons.

I think of Revelation 1:18, NKJV, *"I am He who lives, and was dead, and behold, I am alive forevermore. Amen. And I have the keys of Hades and of Death."*

Our enemy, Satan, no longer has the keys to Hades and Death. If when we die, we are a born-again believer, covered by the blood of Jesus Christ, we cannot be locked up in Hades. I believe like Paul, to be absent from the body is to be present with the Lord. (2 Corinthians 5:8)

Resource for Additional Study

If you would like to study more on the meaning of Ephesians 4:8, check out this link with a multitude of commentaries:
https://biblehub.com/commentaries/ephesians/4-8.htm

"Also you shall observe the Feast of the Harvest of the first fruits of your labors from what you sow in the field; also the Feast of the Ingathering at the end of the year when you gather in the fruit of your labors from the field."

Exodus 23:16, NKJV

Chapter 4

Shavuot, Feast of Weeks, Festival of Reaping, and Pentecost

Shavuot is commonly known in English as the Feast of Weeks or Pentecost.

The Shadow/The Law
Shavuot/Feast of Weeks

The following information is taken from the website: https://www.myjewishlearning.com/article/shavuot-history-from-the-bible-to-temple-times/

"The first thing that one notices with regard to Shavuot in the Bible is the absence of a substantive name for the holiday. Shavuot has several designations in the Bible. The Book of Exodus 23:16 designates it as *"Hag HaKatzir"* — the Festival of the Harvest — which identifies the holiday with an agricultural season. The Book of Numbers 28:26 designates it as *"Hag HaBikkurim"* — the Festival of the First Fruits, which specified the time on which the custom was to offer first fruits.

"The same verse also mentions the name by which the holiday is commonly known today — Shavuot — the Festival of Weeks. This name is not descriptive of the character and substance of the holiday. Rather, it is a chronological tag that addresses itself to the time lapse between Passover and Shavuot, thus emphasizing the relationship and interdependence of the two holidays.

"The agricultural aspect of the holiday began on the second day of Passover and the ritual of the Omer, the offering of a sheaf of barley, the earliest of the new cereal crops, <u>marked the harvest season</u>. The grain ripened 50 days later, thus the beginning of the harvest was marked on Shavuot with the offering of first fruits. This concluded the celebration of the grain <u>harvest</u>, which had begun on the <u>second day of Passover</u>." (Emphasis added)

When looking at Passover, Unleavened Bread, and First Fruits, we see that First Fruits is connected to harvest. The feast is an offering of the first fruits from the harvest.

Feast of Harvest/Pentecost was the celebration of the beginning of the early weeks of harvest, sometime during the middle of the month of May or sometimes in early June. The Feast of First Fruits was the celebration of the beginning of the barley harvest. Pentecost was celebrated 50 days after First Fruits, and 50 days equals seven weeks so it was called the Feast of Harvest or the Feast of Weeks.

The Reality/Grace
Pentecost - Sending the Holy Spirit

The Greek name for Shavuot is Pentecost. Fifty days after The Feast of First Fruits, Shavuot/Pentecost was celebrated.

To understand The Reality/Grace, we need to take a look at those 50 days between the two feasts from the New Testament/New Covenant in the book of Acts.

After Christ was crucified and raised from the dead, He was seen by His disciples. And He actually was seen by approximately 500 people over a period of 40 days before He ascended to the Father (I Corinthians 15:1-11).

In the book of Acts, chapter 1, we see Christ's instructions to His disciples to remain in Jerusalem and wait for the promise.

"...He (Jesus) gave them this command: 'Do not leave Jerusalem, but wait for the gift my Father promised, which you have heard Me speak about. For John baptized with water, but in a few days you will be baptized with the Holy Spirit.'"
Acts 1:4-55, NIV

Jesus instructed them to wait for the promise because they would receive power to take His message to "the ends of the earth."

*"'But you will receive power when the Holy Spirit comes on you; and you will be My witnesses in **Jerusalem**, and in all **Judea** and **Samaria**, and to the **ends of the earth**.' After He said this, He was taken up before their very eyes, and a cloud hid Him from their sight."*
Acts 1:8-9, NIV (Emphasis added)

We learn from verses 13-15, that approximately 120 gathered in an upper room for the next ten days to pray and wait.

On the tenth day since Jesus had ascended, which was the 50th day from the Feast of First Fruits, the day of Shavuot/Feast of Weeks/Feast of Reaping, the promise arrived. We read about it in Acts 2:1-4, NKJV:

"When the Day of Pentecost had fully come, they were all with one accord in one place. And suddenly there came a sound from heaven, as of a rushing mighty wind, and it filled the whole house where they were sitting. Then there appeared to them divided tongues, as of fire, and one sat upon each of them. And they were all filled with the Holy Spirit and began to speak with other tongues, as the Spirit gave them utterance."

When people in the city heard them, they were confused to hear these (possibly uneducated) people speaking in different languages. Peter preached a sermon that touched the hearts of those hearing it. He told them that it was promised by the prophet Joel, and it was now realized at Pentecost.

"Then those who gladly received his word were baptized; and that day about three thousand souls were added to them."
Acts 2:41, NKJV

The known believers went from approximately 120 to approximately 3,120 because of the gospel being preached in the power of the Holy Spirit. And the growth of the church/believers didn't stop there. All through the book of Acts, we see thousands being added and many are still being added today.

Jesus, the First Fruits, marked the beginning of the harvest season, and at Pentecost, the harvest began in Jerusalem and quickly spread throughout the known world. The harvest continues to "the ends of the earth." I am so thankful I am a part of that harvest.

There is also a Feast Sukkoth/Tabernacle/Booths for the latter harvest. I believe the latter harvest represents the time when Jesus will return to gather us to Himself. As the angels said to the disciples in Acts 1:11, NIV, *"...this same Jesus, who has been taken from you into heaven, will come back in the same way you have seen Him go into heaven."*

"The high priest, the one among his brothers who has had the anointing oil poured on his head and who has been ordained to wear the priestly garments..."

Leviticus 21:10, NIV

Chapter 5

High Priest

The Shadow/Law
The High Priest Office

The high priest was the supreme religious leader of the Israelites. The office of the high priest was hereditary and was traced from Aaron, the brother of Moses, of the Levite tribe (Exodus 28:1; Numbers 18:7). The high priest had to be "whole" physically (without any physical defects) and holy in his conduct (Leviticus 21:6-8).

Because the high priest held the leadership position, one of his roles was overseeing the responsibilities of all the subordinate priests (2 Chronicles 19:11). Though the high priest could participate in ordinary priestly ministries, only certain functions were given to him. Only the high priest could wear the Urim and the Thummim.

Urim and Thummim - *noun*
engraved dice-like stones used to determine truth or falsity.

For this reason, the Hebrew people would go to the high priest in order to know the will of God (Numbers 27:21). An example of this is when Joshua was commissioned by Eleazar, the high priest, to assume some of Moses' responsibilities (Numbers 27:21).

The high priest had to offer a sin offering not only for the sins of the whole congregation, but also for himself (Leviticus 4:3-21). When a high priest died, all those confined to the cities of refuge for accidentally causing the death of another person were granted freedom (Numbers 35:28).

The most important duty of the high priest was to conduct the service on the Day of Atonement, the tenth day of the seventh month of every year (Numbers 29:7). Only he was allowed to enter the Most Holy Place behind the veil to stand before God. Having made a sacrifice for himself and for the people, he then brought the blood into the Holy of Holies and sprinkled it on the mercy seat, God's "throne" (Leviticus 16:14-15). He did this to make atonement for himself and the people for all their sins committed during the year just ended (Exodus 30:10).

The High Priest was a mediator between God and man. He was the only person who could approach God for mankind. He was the only one who could take the blood of the animal sacrifice to the Mercy Seat, which was behind the veil in the Most Holy Place.

The veil, sometimes called "the curtain," was very ornate and separated the Holy Place from the Holy of Holies. Some references to the veil/curtain can be found in the Old Covenant, Exodus 26, 27:21, 30:6, 35:12, 36:35, 39:34, 40:3, 21-26; Leviticus 4:6, 17, 16:2, 12-15, 24:3; Numbers 4:5, 18:7; 2 Chronicles 3:14.

God is holy, and mankind is sinful. Thus, there is a need for a mediator between God and mankind—the role of the High Priest. If He had sin and entered the Holy of Holies, he would die.

It is important to note the veil was 60 feet tall and four inches thick and represented the separation of God and mankind. Before Adam sinned in the garden of Eden, scripture tells us that he walked and talked with God. Before the fall, mankind had access to God, but that all changed when sin entered. Someone would have to bring righteousness (right standing with God) back to mankind.

The Reality/Grace
Jesus, Our High Priest

In understanding the role of the high priest, we can better comprehend the significance of Christ offering Himself for our sins once for all (Hebrews 9:26; 10:10, 12). Through Christ's sacrifice for us, we are sanctified and set apart for Him. By entering God's presence on our behalf, Christ has secured for us an "eternal redemption" (Hebrews 9:12). As Paul has written,

"For there is one God, and there is one mediator between God and men, the man
Christ Jesus"
1 Timothy 2:5

The High Priest had to be whole with no defects and holy in his conduct. Jesus, our High Priest, fulfilled this as He was the only one without sin. (I Peter 1:19, 2 Corinthians 5:21)

The High Priest had the leadership position/authority overseeing the responsibility of all other priests. Jesus, our High Priest, fulfills this every day. He has complete authority over all of us who are following Him, who have been made priests in His kingdom (Revelation 1:6, Revelation 5:10, Revelation 20:6, I Peter 2:5, I Peter 2:9).

"Not that we are competent in ourselves to claim anything for ourselves, but our
competence comes from God. He has made us competent as ministers of a new

The High Priest would seek the will of God for the people. In the New Testament, we find a reference to the high priest having the gift of prophecy (John 11:49-52). Jesus fulfills this as He and the Father are One, and He knows the will of the Father. (John 10:30, John 4:34, John 6:38)

The High Priest in the Old Testament had to offer sacrifices for his sins and the sins of the people. Jesus was without sin, and He did offer Himself as a sacrifice for our sins. (John 3:16, I John 2:2, Romans 5:8)

When the High Priest died, all those confined to the cities of refuge were set free. With Christ's sacrifice, death, resurrections, mankind can be freed from what has kept them bound. (John 8:32, 36)

The High Priest's most important duty was on the Day of Atonement, taking the blood of the animal sacrifice into the Most Holy Place. Jesus fulfilled this by His blood sacrifice for the remission of our sins. (Hebrews 9:12)

The High Priest was a mediator between God and man. Jesus fulfills this by being our mediator. There is only one mediator between God and man in the New Covenant. (I Timothy 2:5)

Only the High Priest could go behind the veil into the presence of God. Jesus fulfilled this in that, while He was on the cross, the veil was ripped from top to bottom, now opening up our way to go boldly before the throne of God. We can now talk with God seven days a week, 24 hours a day. (Matthew 27:50-51, Hebrews 4:16)

The book of Hebrews is chock full of information on Jesus becoming our High Priest. I'm going to share a few scriptures from Hebrews, but I suggest that you do your own study of Hebrews.

"Therefore, in all things He had to be made like His brethren, that He might be a merciful and faithful High Priest in things pertaining to God, to make propitiation for the sins of the people."
Hebrews 2:17, NIV

"Jesus has become the guarantee of a better covenant … because Jesus lives forever, He has a permanent priesthood. Therefore He is able to save **completely** *those who come to God through Him, because He always lives to intercede for them."*
Hebrews 7:22-25, NIV (Emphasis added)

"Unlike the other high priests, He does not need to offer sacrifices day after day, first for His own sins, and then for the sins of the people. He sacrificed for their sins once for all when He offered Himself. For the law appoints as high priests men in all their weakness; but the oath, which came after the law, appointed the Son, who has been made perfect forever."
Hebrews 7:27-28, NIV

*"For Christ is not entered into the Holy places made with hands, which are the **figures** of the true; but into heaven itself,
to appear in the presence of God for us."*

Hebrews 9:24 (Emphasis added)

Chapter 6

Mary and Elizabeth, John the Baptist and Jesus

I believe this New Testament reality was actually in two phases. The first is mentioned in Luke.

"At that time Mary got ready and hurried to a town in the hill country of Judea, where she entered Zechariah's home and greeted Elizabeth. When Elizabeth heard Mary's greeting, the baby leaped in her womb, and Elizabeth was filled with the Holy Spirit. In a loud voice she exclaimed: 'Blessed are you among women, and blessed is the child you will bear! But why am I so favored, that the mother of my Lord should come to me? As soon as the sound of your greeting reached my ears, the baby in my womb leaped for joy. Blessed is she who has believed that the Lord would fulfill His promises to her!'"
Luke 1:39-45, NIV

I have often wondered about Mary's visit to Elizabeth. I have heard ministers say that they were cousins—close cousins—even first cousins. But I could never reconcile that because Elizabeth was of the tribe of Levi, from the priestly family of Aaron as was her husband. And Mary was of the tribe of Judah, King David's family. So, at best, they were very distant cousins since Levi and Judah were brothers, but at this time it is approximately 1,700 years later. (The King James Bible says "cousin" but this is not correct.)

From *Dake Annotated Reference Bible KJV*, "The Greek word *subgenus,* means "countryman," not cousin in the sense we use it. And this word is used only in Luke 1:36 and in Luke 1:58.

I have wondered why Mary would go visit Elizabeth. Elizabeth was much older and had conceived in her later years, she was six months pregnant with John the Baptist when Mary visited. This journey was approximately 80 to 100 miles. Mary was young (some believe as young as 14) and had conceived by the Holy Spirit. Did the Holy Spirit instruct Mary to visit Elizabeth? Did Mary know her? Was Elizabeth a friend of Mary's mother? We really don't know the answers. However, I tend to believe that it was the Holy Spirit directing Mary to visit Elizabeth. Elizabeth was going to be used to prophesy to Mary about the son Mary would give birth to.

There is so much more to this story than I have ever thought about before and I have never heard anyone preach or teach on this.

It wasn't until March 6, 2023, while studying the book of Hebrews, I believe revelation knowledge came to me. I was studying Jesus as our High Priest and replacing the old order of the priesthood. The encounter between Mary and Elizabeth had a much deeper meaning than I had ever thought about before. Elizabeth was of the old priesthood family and Mary was giving birth to the new priesthood.

Then I thought about John the Baptist, who was Elizabeth's son. He was also of the old priesthood family, and Jesus came to be **our new high priest**. When John the Baptist said (John 3:20) *"I must decrease* *and HE must increase,"* I believe John was speaking about the **old** (priesthood) coming to an end and the **new** beginning. John, representing the old priesthood, was preparing the way for the new priesthood in Jesus, the Messiah.

I personally believe when John baptized Jesus, it was showing the passing of the priesthood. John did not want to baptize Jesus, but Jesus said it had to be done to fulfill the law's requirements or righteousness.

*"Then Jesus came from Galilee to John at the Jordan to be baptized by him. And "John tried to prevent Him, saying, 'I need to be baptized by You, and are You coming to me?' But Jesus answered and said to him, 'Permit it to be so now, for thus it is fitting for us to **fulfill all righteousness.** *' Then he allowed Him. When He had been baptized, Jesus came up immediately from the water; and behold, the heavens were opened to Him, and he saw the Spirit of God descending like a dove and alighting upon Him. And suddenly a voice came from heaven, saying, 'This is My beloved Son, in whom I am well pleased.'"*
Matthew 3:13-17, NKJV (Emphasis added)

There was a passing of the priesthood from one to another.

*"not in the order of Aaron. For when there is a change of the priesthood, there must be a change of the law. He of whom these things are said belonged to a **different tribe, and no one from that tribe has ever served at the altar.** For it is clear that our Lord descended from Judah, and in regard to that tribe Moses said nothing about priests… One who has become a priest not on the basis of a regulation as to His ancestry but on the basis of the power of an indestructible life."*
Hebrews 7:11-14,16, NIV (Emphasis added)

The second phase, I believe, is how Jesus fulfills the office of High

Priest, mentioned in the previous chapter.

---

*From The Translators New Testament, verse 15, *"for in this way it is fitting for us to fulfill all that God requires."*

"*Jesus saith unto him, 'I am the way, the truth, and the life: no man cometh unto the Father, but by Me.'*"

John 14:6

"*Salvation is found in no one else, for there is no other name under heaven given to mankind by which we must be saved.*"

Acts 4:12, NIV

Epilogue

As mentioned at the beginning of this book, I have not attempted to cover all of the types and shadows from the Old Covenant/The Law and fulfilled in the New Covenant/Grace—that book would be much larger than this one. These brief chapters are meant to provide a small understanding of how Jesus fulfilled the Old and established the New.

In addition to sharing these, I also want to share with you how Jesus fulfilled the prophecies in the Old Covenant.

In the spring of 2006, my siblings and I had the task of cleaning out our mother's home. She could no longer live by herself and was being moved into our oldest brother's home. She was suffering from the dreaded disease, Alzheimer's. Mom had been an avid reader, student of the scriptures, and teacher at her local church for years. As we were going through her things, I came across a book by Dr. D. James Kennedy titled *Why I Believe*.

I was intrigued and wanted this book to take back to my home library. I was somewhat familiar with Dr. Kennedy having gone through his course *Evangelism Explosion* at my local church. I was not disappointed. I love this book and have been able to teach Bible studies from it.

I now want to share some of the wonderful nuggets that Dr. Kennedy shares in his book, in the chapter *Why I Believe in Jesus*.

In addition to the writers of the Gospels, many secular historians and Jewish writers have written about Jesus: Pontius Pilate, Thallus, and Tacitius, just to name a few.

The Old Testament includes about 60 different prophecies, with more than 300 references of the coming Messiah (Anointed One).

These are specific prophecies, not generalities:

1) He would be a leader/prophet like Moses.
2) He would be a descendant of Noah's son, Shem.
3) He would be a descendant of Shem through Abraham.
4) He would be a descendant of Abraham's son Isaac.
5) He would be a descendant of Isaac's son Jacob.
6) He would be a descendant of Jacob's son Judah.
7) He would be a descendant of the family of Jesse.
8) He would be of the house of David.
9) He would be born in Bethlehem.
10) He would be born of a virgin.
11) He would come while the Temple of Jerusalem was still standing (destroyed in 70 A.D.).
12) He would perform many miracles.
13) He would speak in parables.
14) The Gentiles would believe in Him while His own people (the Jews) reject Him.
15) A messenger (a man in the wilderness—John the Baptist) would prepare the way.

The prophecies about Jesus in the Old Testament are so specific. It not only records that He would be betrayed, but it would be by someone He considered to be His friend. It also records how much money that friend would get for his betrayal—30 pieces of silver (Zechariah 11:12-13)—and that the money would ultimately be used to buy a potter's field.

Not only was His birth prophesied but His death was prophesied in great detail.

A number of years ago, Peter W. Stoner and Robert C. Newman wrote a book entitled *Science Speaks.* The book was based on the science of probability and vouched for by American Scientific Affiliation. It set out the odds of any one man in all of history fulfilling even only eight of the 60 major prophecies (and 270 ramifications) fulfilled by the life of Christ.

The probability that Jesus of Nazareth could have fulfilled even eight such prophecies would be only 1 in 10 to the 17th power. That is 1 in 100,000,000,000,000,000.

To better understand this number, Stoner claims that 10 to the 17th power in silver dollars would be enough to cover the face of the entire state of Texas two feet deep. Texas is a very large state and it takes a long time to drive across it. The probability of Jesus fulfilling all of these prophecies by chance is like blindfolding a man, setting him out of Dallas on foot, letting him go in any direction, and on the very first attempt, picking up one specifically marked silver dollar out of 100,000,000,000,000,000.

Richard Haverson, then Chaplain of the United States Senate, wrote this:

"The fact is, the birth, crucifixion and bodily resurrection of Jesus Christ are celebrated worldwide by folk of every race, language, and color, every year. And by believing in Jesus, they have been delivered from the most evil, disastrous, frustrating, debilitating habits and life forms possible. The real problem with Jesus Christ is not that folk can't believe in Him—but that they won't believe in Him."

Oftentimes, when I have personally encountered people who want to question the deity of Jesus and what proof I have of who He is, this is what I share. The life of Christ changed our world and even the way we tell time - B.C. (Before Christ) and A.D. (Latin - Anno Domini, which means "In the year of our Lord"). There is no other so-called "god," man, celebrity, etc. that has ever done that.

Jesus declared seven times in the Gospel of John, "I AM."

- John 6:35, "the Bread of Life"
- John 8:12, "the Light of the World"
- John 10:9, "the Gate"
- John 10:11, "the Good Shepherd"
- John 11:25, "the Resurrection and the Life"
- John 14:6, "the Way and the Truth and the Life"
- John 15:1, "the True Vine"

"I AM" Hebrew grammar here means: "I AM" - "I WAS" - and "I WILL BE." He is, He always was, and He always will be.

"Jesus Christ is the same yesterday, today, and forever."
Hebrews 13:8, NKJV

***

If you have never made Jesus the Lord of your life, you can right now. By praying a simple prayer:

1) Asking to be forgiven for your sins.
2) Declaring that you believe Jesus is the Son of God,

3) That He was born of a virgin,

4) He died on the cross and shed His blood for the remission of your sins,

5) that He arose from the dead and is now seated at the right-hand (place of authority) of the throne of God making intercession for you,

`6) and it is by Him, and only by Him that you can have salvation.

"if you confess with your mouth that Jesus is Lord and believe in your heart that God raised Him from the dead, you will be saved."
Romans 10:9, ESV

If you sincerely prayed this prayer you can know for a certainty that you are saved. He promised us in His word.

"For I will forgive their evildoing and remember their sins no more."
Hebrews 8:12, NAB

"as far as the east is from the west, so far does He remove our transgressions from us."
Psalm 103:12, ESV

When you accept Jesus as your Lord and Savior, you are like a little baby and you need to thrive in your new life. In order to do that, you need nourishment. You need to be in a Bible-believing, preaching, and teaching church. You need to develop a habit of reading your Bible every day while praying and asking the Holy Spirit to open up your understanding into the ways of God.

Please tell someone. You can write to us or send us an email. Please be sure to tell your pastor.

"Jesus Christ is the same yesterday, today, and forever."

Hebrews 13:8, NKJV

Appendix

Jesus in Every Book of the Bible

The following list is from:

https://www.gotquestions.org/Jesus-in-every-book-of-the-Bible.html

It shows Jesus in every book of the Bible. I have divided the list showing the Old Testament from the New Testament. I believe this shows the "Shadow or Type" in the Old Testament and the "Reality" in the New Testament.

He is The Alpha and the Omega, the Beginning and the End, and He is coming again and the One who makes all things new.

Old Testament/Covenant – The Shadow

- **Genesis** — Jesus is the Word of God, creating the heavens and the earth. He is the promised "seed of the woman."
- **Exodus** — Jesus is the Passover lamb.
- **Leviticus** — Jesus is the high priest and representative of the tabernacle. He is the lampstand, the showbread, and the sacrifice on the altar.
- **Numbers** — Jesus is the pillar of cloud by day and the pillar of fire by night and the smitten rock that gives living water.
- **Deuteronomy** — Jesus is the prophet greater than Moses.

- **Joshua** — Jesus is the commander of the army of the Lord, leading His people into the Promised Land.
- **Judges** — Jesus is the true and final judge.
- **Ruth** — Jesus is the kinsman redeemer.
- **1 & 2 Samuel** — Jesus is the anointed shepherd king who slays the giant.
- **1 & 2 Kings** — Jesus is the righteous King of Kings and Lord of Lords.
- **1 & 2 Chronicles** — Jesus is the faithful restorer of the kingdom.
- **Ezra** — Jesus is the faithful restorer of the temple.
- **Nehemiah** — Jesus is the redeeming rebuilder of the walls.
- **Esther** — Jesus is the sovereign protector of His people.
- **Job** — Jesus is the living redeemer and our true comforter.
- **Psalms** — Jesus is the Good Shepherd who hears our cries.
- **Proverbs** — Jesus is wisdom.
- **Ecclesiastes** — Jesus is the meaning of life.
- **Song of Solomon** — Jesus is the loving bridegroom coming for His bride.
- **Isaiah** — Jesus is the promised Messiah, the Wonderful Counselor, Mighty God, Everlasting Father, Prince of Peace, and Suffering Servant wounded for our transgression and bruised for our iniquities.
- **Jeremiah** — Jesus is the potter and the Righteous Branch.
- **Lamentations** — Jesus is the weeping prophet.
- **Ezekiel** — Jesus is the river of life, bringing healing to the nations.
- **Daniel** — Jesus is the fourth man in the fiery furnace.
- **Hosea** — Jesus is the ever-faithful husband pursuing His unfaithful bride.
- **Joel** — Jesus is the restorer of what the locusts have eaten and the one who will pour His Spirit on His people.

- **Amos** — Jesus is the burden-bearer and the true restoration.
- **Obadiah** — Jesus is the judge of all the earth and mighty to save.
- **Jonah** — Jesus is the salvation of all lands and the prophet cast out in the storm who spent three days in the depths.
- **Micah** — Jesus is the promised Messiah born in Bethlehem.
- **Nahum** — Jesus is the avenger of God's elect.
- **Habakkuk** — Jesus is the reason for rejoicing and our strength even when the fields are empty.
- **Zephaniah** — Jesus is the preserver and restorer of His remnant and kingdom.
- **Haggai** — Jesus is the desire of all nations.
- **Zechariah** — Jesus is the cleansing fountain and the pierced Son whom every eye on earth will one day behold.
- **Malachi** — Jesus is the Sun of Righteousness, rising with healing in His wings; He is the refiner's fire.

New Testament/Covenant – The Reality

- **Matthew** — Jesus is the King of the Jews.
- **Mark** — Jesus is the Servant King.
- **Luke** — Jesus is the Son of Man.
- **John** — Jesus is the Son of God, the Word made flesh who dwelt among us, and the Lamb of God who takes away the sins of the world.
- **Acts** — Jesus is the risen Lord, bringing salvation to all nations.
- **Romans** — Jesus is our justification and the righteousness of God.
- **1 Corinthians** — Jesus is the Rock.
- **2 Corinthians** — Jesus is our triumph, sanctifying the church.

- Galatians — Jesus is the liberation that fulfills the law and sets us free.
- Ephesians — Jesus is the head of the church who gives us God's armor.
- Philippians — Jesus is our joy.
- Colossians — Jesus is the firstborn of all creation and the head of the church.
- 1 Thessalonians — Jesus is coming again with a trumpet and a shout to meet believers in the clouds.
- 2 Thessalonians — Jesus is believers' patience as they await His return.
- 1 Timothy — Jesus is our mediator between God and man.
- 2 Timothy — Jesus is the Seed of David, raised from the dead, and our salvation.
- Titus — Jesus is our blessed hope and our faithful pastor.
- Philemon — Jesus is our Redeemer, restoring us to effective service.
- Hebrews — Jesus is our High Priest and the author and finisher of our faith.
- James — Jesus is the One at work in our faith in action.
- 1 Peter — Jesus is the Living Stone, the Chief Cornerstone, and the Rock of Offense.
- 2 Peter — Jesus is the faithful, longsuffering Lord, not willing that any should perish but offering salvation to all.
- 1 John — Jesus is love and the true and eternal God.
- 2 John — Jesus is the truth by which we walk in love.
- 3 John — Jesus is all that is good and a hospitable host.
- Jude — Jesus is the One who keeps us from stumbling and presents us blameless with great joy.
- Revelation — Jesus is the Alpha and Omega, the beginning and end, the Lamb slain before the foundation of the world, the King of Kings and Lord of Lords.

About the Author

Reverend Jesten Peters
Keys of Authority Ministries, Inc.

Reverend Peters has been saved and serving the Lord for over 65 years. Feeling she was called to ministry, Jesten sought formal training at *Central Bible College* (Detroit extension campus), *RHEMA Bible College*, Broken Arrow, Oklahoma, earned a Bachelor of Theology degree in 2001 and a Master of Theology degree in 2013 from *International Seminary* in Florida. She was licensed for ministry in 1982, and received her ordination from Seminary in 2001.

Jesten currently travels and ministers through *Keys of Authority Ministries*, which she founded in 2005, and serves as president.

The mission of *Keys of Authority Ministries* and Reverend Peters is to provide teaching to help Christians grow up in their walk with the Lord, by:

1) laying a foundation of percept upon precept and line upon line of the Word of God

2) preparing our hearts to be good ground to receive the Word of God

3) taking the keys of the Word of God into our lives.

Reverend Peters has had numerous articles published in *The Spirit Newspaper*, *New Beginning of Life* Christian magazine, her former church's newsletter, a letter to the editor of *Charisma* Magazine, is the author of *Running to Win the Race* published in 2012 by WestBow Press, *superabundantly more than all that we dare ask or think or DREAM* published in 2018 by Spiritfire Publishing, re-released in 2020 by Keys of Authority Ministries Publishing, and *Nothing Can Separate Us From The Love of God* published in 2020, by Keys of Authority Ministries Publishing. Jesten is also a contributing writer to *We May Be Done, But We're Not Finished!* released in the Summer of 2021.

She occasionally writes articles for the Faith section of her local newspaper *The Palatka Daily News*, and writes daily devotions for the ministry Facebook page.

Additionally, Jesten has received the following awards and has been recognized in the following areas:

1) received the key to the City of Eatonton, Georgia in connection with her prison ministry work in middle Georgia in the 1980's

2) received a plaque in 2001 from *International Seminary* in recognition of 35 years of gospel ministry

3) named "2005 Woman of the Year" for Columbia County, Florida

4) named one of "2012's 8 Phenomenal Women" by *RENEWED Magazine* Special Women's Issue Summer 2012

5) received a plaque in 2013 from *International Seminary* in recognition of 48 years of gospel ministry

6) honored by being featured in *Women of Distinction Magazine,* Spring 2017

For more information on Reverend Peters and the ministry, please visit the website at:

www.keysofauthorityministries.org